Sex

We live under a cheerful delusion that sex might nowadays be easy – because we have been 'liberated' from the hang-ups and taboos of the olden days. Yet nothing could be further from the truth. Despite a veneer of openness, sex remains an extraordinarily complicated business, hard to discuss and surrounded by shame and unspoken desires. This book provides a relief from the loneliness and confusion, explaining how sex truly operates and what it aims at. The book demonstrates that far from thinking about sex too much, we haven't begun to think about it as deeply as we should.

Published in 2017 by The School of Life
70 Marchmont Street, London WC1N 1AB
Copyright © The School of Life 2017
Designed and typeset by FLOK, Berlin
Printed in Latvia by Livonia Print

A proportion of this book has appeared online at thebookoflife.org.

The School of Life offers programmes, publications and services to
assist modern individuals in their quest to live more engaged and
meaningful lives. We've also developed a collection of content-rich,
design-led retail products to promote useful insights and ideas from
culture.

www.theschooloflife.com

978-0-9935387-6-6

Sex

THE SCHOOL OF LIFE

Contents

3 Conclusion

1

Introduction

i. Liberation and Non-Liberation

There is a curious and disturbing fact about human nature: we have different sides to our characters, and different needs, some of which seem notably high-minded and others notably 'low'. We can see the division in dramatic instances: a person delivering a lecture on the meaning of life may be seized by an urgent need to burp; we might try hard to eat a sensible diet, then give way to a craving for confectionary late at night.

We have different words to capture these divisions: the animal and the human; reason and passion; the beast and the angel. So different are these sides, it can seem as if each individual were really two warring people trapped within the same skin.

Nowhere does this contrast feel more intense than around sex. The English novelist Kingsley Amis (1922–1995) commented in old age on having had an active libido: *for 50 years it was like being chained to an idiot.*

Generally, we're deeply invested in the idea of love. We want to be close, tender and sweet with partners, meet their needs and take their interests to heart. But our libido often doesn't agree: it just wants maximum excitement in a variety of immediate, ruthless and disembodied ways. We may try hard to be polite and considerate to others, but our sex drive may be eager to tie a partner up and flog them. Normally we may be very concerned about our own dignity and feel affronted if another person violates our personal space, while around sex we might be keen to have our genitals roughly explored. One minute, we're fussily wiping a tiny spot from the kitchen work surface; at another point, we may be content to defile and be defiled.

When we reflect on these divisions in ourselves, the instinctive response is shame. The nice side of our nature – the side committed to dignity, respect and status – can feel deeply awkward about being tethered to an apparently delinquent persona.

However, the sense that we need to hide, deny and bury key elements of who we are is not very good for us. As psychoanalysis has stressed, when we repress things that are important, they make themselves heard in other ways. The 'dirty' parts of ourselves can show up disguised as greed, harsh opinions, bad temper, the longing to boss other people about, alcoholism or other forms of risky, damaging behaviour. Freud's lasting contribution was to put his finger on the cost of disavowing powerful parts of ourselves.

There have been occasional attempts to reconcile our inner conflicts. The French philosopher Michel de Montaigne (1533–1592) was keen to point out how even the most elevated and respected people shared a common basic nature – and he formulated striking aphorisms to stress the point: 'Kings and philosophers shit and so do ladies'. And: 'Even on the highest

throne in the world we are seated still upon our arses.'
If we smile at a learned and serious character like
Montaigne making these remarks, it stems from relief
at encountering a kindly, generous voice acknowledg-
ing what we cannot normally face.

Shame around sex has a long history. In much of the
world, for long periods, anal sex between men was
the cause of such concern that it was declared illegal.
In England, Henry VIII signed The Buggery Act in
1533. The original punishment for this was hanging;
in 1861, this was reduced merely to imprisonment. It
was not until 1967 that homosexual acts (in private)
stopped being against the law.

Many societies have sought to dampen sexual desire
by encouraging people to don clothes designed to
repel erotic curiosity. In the 1830s in the UK, gen-
teel ladies were encouraged to cover as much of the
body as possible in voluminous dresses, headscarves
and gloves; giving a glimpse of so much as an ankle
was considered scandalous. In Islam, the hijab was
introduced to prevent men getting overexcited by the
sight of a woman's neck. The very language we have
inherited is full of euphemism that skirts around the
explicit description of things we might do with our
bodies. 'Adult films' do not refer to the works of the
Russian director Andrei Tarkovsky.

Our shame might sit oddly with us because, at another level, we've taken to heart the idea that we live

in an era of sexual liberation. It may be true that in recent decades, a degree of progress has been made. Stand-up comics can make jokes about masturbation; women's sexual appetites have been recognised; bathrooms are designed to feel airy and open. Yet the notion that we are liberated causes us problems all of its own, because it brings with it the assumption that hang-ups and awkwardness can no longer legitimately exist.

In truth, real liberation remains a radically unfinished project; 'unfinished' because we continue to struggle to admit some key things about who we are from a sexual perspective. There is still a very strong presumption that all decent relationships must be monogamous. We retain a strong ideal of being 'respectable'. There's a powerful presumption that (for instance) a married mother of two who works as a procurement manager for a pharmaceutical firm won't regularly visit sex clubs; that a tax specialist won't be wearing fetish clothing under their suit at an important meeting with clients; that a senior politician won't spend a lot of their free time watching pornography – if it turned out they did, it might cause a huge scandal. A lot of quite normal aspects of human sexuality remain located outside our well-intentioned but punitive and normative rules.

The current taboos around sex have their roots in an unfortunate movement of ideas, which can be broadly termed Romanticism, that originated in Europe in the late 18th century. A central aspect of Romanticism is the notion that sex must be interpreted as the ultimate expression of love. According to Romanticism, to love is to feel infinitely sweet towards one's beloved, to be gentle and delicate around them and to renounce interest in all others. The Romantics turned sex into the crowning moment of love, and deemed unacceptable any kind of sexual activity that couldn't be tethered to a sincere expression of affection.

This is a touching idea, but it has ushered in appalling problems: sex and Romantic love can only ever overlap in part and from time to time, while the precarious, fragile ideal of their perfect conjunction has come to be regarded, emotionally speaking, as a necessity.

Sexual self-acceptance does not have to mean abandoning all control or the deliberate flaunting of our less elevated needs at every turn. We don't have to fully embrace every impulse; we just need to be able to admit, in an unfrightened way, that they exist. Just because – as Montaigne knew – we shit, it doesn't mean we don't have bathroom doors. There's still a central place for restraint and politeness. However, the core point of true liberation is to reduce the unfair and debilitating burden of shame with which we continue to wrestle.

ii. What This Book Is For

Shame means that many couples still find it difficult to be honest with one another about who they are and what they need to feel satisfied. This cuts them off from sources of affection and honesty. Sexual loneliness remains a norm.

We shouldn't suppose that we can always and invariably share our every sexual proclivity with others, but there's a lot we could feel more confident about expressing. Things that seem strange can turn out to be quite understandable when we consider them rationally; there's an important role for philosophical analysis in stretching the understanding we have of our own desires.

This is where we locate the purpose of this book: we explore a range of sexual enthusiasms in order to help us acknowledge hitherto forbidden aspects of ourselves and to communicate them in unpanicked, undefensive ways to our partners. Our goal is to help us to be maturely unfrightened of our own sexuality; to reduce unnecessary shame; and to increase opportunities for moments of courageous and relationship-enhancing honesty.

2

Our Sexual Desires

i. Kissing

Mutual desire is normally signalled by a pretty weird act; two organs otherwise used for eating and speaking are rubbed and pressed against one another with increasing force, accompanied by the secretion of saliva. A tongue normally precisely manipulated to articulate vowel sounds, or to push mashed potato or broccoli to the rear of the palate now moves forward to meet its counterpart, whose tip it might touch in repeated staccato movements. One would have to carefully explain to an alien visitor from Kepler 9b what is going on. They are not about to bite chunks out of each other's cheeks; nor are they attempting to inflate another person.

Why is kissing so significant and potentially so exciting? It seems odd to point it out, although it is crucial: from a purely physical point of view, kissing is not an especially pleasant experience. To press one's lips against those of another person is not a remarkably more enjoyable tactile feeling than having a scalp massage or eating an oyster. To lick another person's teeth or tongue delivers only a modest burst of positive sensory stimulation. Yet kissing can be one of the nicest things we ever do.

The reason for this is that kissing can deliver a major psychological thrill. The pleasure we experience has its origin in the idea of being allowed to do a very private thing to and with another person. Another person's mouth is a highly protected and private zone. It would be deeply offensive to go up to a stranger and finger their cheeks and lips. So it is truly remarkable to be allowed to get one's face extremely close to that of another and to actually slide one's tongue inside their head.

It could so easily be revolting, and yet isn't, which is what is so exciting. The mutual permission involved in a kiss is dramatic and large. We're implicitly saying to another person through our kiss that they have been placed in a tiny, intensely privileged category of people. There's a special joy in touching someone's back teeth with your tongue that has nothing to do with the appeal of licking enamel. To allow someone to do these things signals a huge level of acceptance, and this is what is thrilling.

Sexual excitement is psychological. It's not so much what our bodies are doing that gets us turned on; it's what happens in our brains that matters. Although we don't normally spell it out – so it can sound a bit strange – acceptance is at the centre of the kinds of experiences we collectively refer to as 'getting turned on'. It feels physical – the blood pumps faster, the metabolism shifts gear, the skin gets hot. However, behind all this lies a very different kind of change that could grandly, but appropriately, be described as metaphysical because it concerns the basic feature of our mode of being human: the relationship between the Self and the Other.

Normally, the self is separate and apart. We're deeply conscious of the distance between our own existence and that of everyone else. There's a permanent undercurrent of isolation, touchingly expressed by the British poet Matthew Arnold (1822–1888):

> In the sea of life enisled,
> With echoing straits between us thrown,
> Dotting the shoreless watery wild,
> We mortal millions live alone.

Arnold was developing a visual metaphor to sum up our sense that between us and other people there lies:

> The unplumbed, salt, estranging sea.

Apart from the public overt person, everyone has a more elusive, deeper self, which is kept in reserve as far as other people are concerned, and yet is hugely familiar from the inside. There are so many thoughts and desires that circulate through our minds that we need to keep gently concealed from other people – because of a very natural and reasonable sense of how upsetting they would be if made public. The inner lives of others are hinted at, sometimes in very confusing ways, by their words and actions. Mostly we don't really know what is going on for them. We long to be accepted, to be close to others, to be open and for them to be open with us – but it feels risky and unavailable, and we fear their negative reactions. The world feels Other and the Self is lonely.

All of us suffer from strong feelings of unacceptability and shame that another person's kiss starts to work on overcoming. This deeper, private self is active in a serious kiss, which is what you feel you are getting and giving access to. In the kiss, our mouth becomes a privileged place in which we surrender our defences and gift ourselves to another. We are exposed and raw.

Kissing promises something more exciting than sex: a brief respite from loneliness. By being in another's mouth, we are signalling a mutual readiness to let the boundaries slip. The actions of our lips and tongues are outward signs of a more momentous inward shift: *I accept you – accept you so much that I will take a big risk with you.* Sexual excitement is the loneliness of the Self powerfully, if briefly, alleviated.

ii. Blushing

One of the odd things that can happen when we feel aroused and excited by the idea of getting together with someone is that we start to blush. Maybe we've been having dinner with a new friend. We're getting more and more turned on. But instead of this making us feel confident and sure of ourselves – instead of easing into a polished, playful response – we find ourselves growing increasingly quiet and reserved, awkward and uncertain. The blood starts to pump into the little capillaries of our cheeks and to our horror we realise that we are starting to blush; a deeply embarrassing crimson flush, which the lovely person sitting opposite surely can't fail to notice. We may think we are turning off our potential partner but, for some very good reasons, blushing can be a highly gratifying phenomenon to witness and to have provoked.

Our tendency to blush speaks of how aware we are that we might be bothering someone with our presence. It is a thrill at the possibility of acceptance mingled with shame at the danger of rejection. To know we might be bothering someone, to hold open the possibility that our advances might be unwelcome, is a highly ethical achievement. It is based upon an acute interest in the minds of others, combined with a deep respect for the ways we might offend and bore. The shy person is touchingly, and in many senses rightly, alive to the dangers of being a nuisance.

Someone with no capacity to blush is, for that reason, a scary possibility; they must operate with a dismaying attitude of entitlement. They can be so composed and sure only because they haven't taken on board the crucial possibility of their unenchanting nature.

Excessive self-doubt and timidity can, of course, blight our lives. But it seems on the edge of something properly worth celebrating: an awareness of how inconvenient we can be to others – an imaginative exercise that helps to keep our unappealing sides usefully in check. The more we understand ourselves, and are honest about our pockets of inadequacy, our capacity to get stumped by small difficulties, our weirder enthusiasms, our oddities and points of raw sensitivity – the bigger a deal it should seem to be embraced by another person. The better we know ourselves, the more amazing it must seem that anyone could ever want to take us on. Shyness is evidence of high degrees of self-knowledge.

Instead of being put out by the fumbling partner across the table or the person sitting primly on the sofa beside us, we should therefore keep open the thought that they may be filled with longing and yearning for intimacy while simply too self-aware to assume that we might be interested in their existence. The capacity to blush is, in its own way, a sign of a deeply evolved and ethical personality. No wonder it may prove such a turn-on.

iii. Keeping Our Clothes On

There is an assumption that sexiness is about nakedness and explicitness, and that logically, therefore,
the sexiest scenarios must also be the ones involving
the greatest amounts of nudity. But the truth about
excitement is likely to be rather different. At the core
of sexiness is the idea of being allowed into someone's
life, when the memory of having been excluded from
it is at its most vivid. Sexiness stems from a contrast
between prohibition and acceptance. It is a species of
relief and thanks at being given permission to enter
another person's life.

We tend to know the thrill of getting sexual while
keeping our clothes on in the earliest days of a relationship. After a party, with neither of us entirely sure
where things are headed, we lie on the bed together
fully clothed and kiss and hug awkwardly.

At these moments, any chance to touch feels deeply
special. A shoulder slipping out from its cardigan cov-
ering, a finger probing the flesh under the waistband
of a skirt, loosening a tie and undoing some buttons
to reveal the neck and the top of the chest: these
things make the permission of bodily discovery very
vivid and powerful. At such moments our excitement
is intimately tethered to gratitude – we realise how
generous the other person has been in allowing us to
roam over their body.

This gratitude is usually most keenly felt not when one has been granted full licence by someone, but when one is on the borderline, when one has only just been lent a pass – and when the memory of the taboo of sex that surrounds most people is still intense. The reminder of the danger of rejection brings the wonder at being included into sharp, ecstatic relief.

As we get used to having sex with someone, it generally happens that their mere nakedness (which was once mysterious and desperately longed for) diminishes quite substantially in its power to excite us. We lose sight of what previously we knew so well: the marvel of acceptance.

This explains why the decision to keep clothes on a bit longer than strictly necessary, to deliberately retain clothes during sex even after the early period, can prove such a turn-on. To heighten excitement, we may design a scenario in which we are 'allowed' only to press against one another, never moving beyond guilty caresses and small thrusts – like we might have been forced to do in early adolescence or in a bedroom in Saudi Arabia. Such games mean we can keep revisiting the incredible idea of permission: the outer garments evoke the barriers one has finally been able to cross with impunity. Playfully limiting oneself to pressing through wool and cotton brings into enticing alignment both one's previous exclusion and the new wondrous inclusion. The rule that we know full well is fake ('don't go too far') makes our status as actual lovers all the more vivid and hence arousing. We are, via the game, trying to recover gratitude.

Prudishness can be willingly invited into our sexual games as a way of reminding us of our enormous, but too often forgotten privileges.

iv. Outdoor Sex

Why should the idea of sex outside be exciting given how awkward, scratchy, sandy or muddy it can be on a beach, halfway up a hillside or in the shady bushes of a park, compared with the comfort of cotton sheets and a sprung mattress?

It's easy to think of orgasms as just physiological phenomena, but really these are manifestations of extreme psychological delight at certain deeply exciting ideas. With outdoor sex, the pleasing, almost utopian, concept driving our pleasure forward is that we could be in a public place where others might see us but that this wouldn't – as it so often does – matter any more. Wrapped up in the throes of passion, protected by the other's desire, the promise is that we could lose self-consciousness and inhibition and entirely reconcile the private and the public sides of ourselves. As we strip each other off in a glade or by the side of a supermarket, there's a refusal to give way to the normal pulses of debilitating shame and embarrassment. Since early adolescence, we have learned to lock doors and keep curtains shut. We have blushed at the threat of exposure. And yet now we're no longer bothered by the sounds of passing traffic or the call of an insistent flock of starlings overhead. Emboldened by another's affection, we are empowered to think that the erotic parts of ourselves don't need to be sheltered and repressed. The outdoor orgasm that culminates signals our pleasure at finally evading our usual self-consciousness.

It should be no surprise that many artists have been
alive to the pleasures of sex outdoors. Think of the
works of the 18th-century French artists Fragonard
and Boucher. To view their canvases is a chance to
turn over in our imagination the luxury and ease of
the Garden of Eden, for which each one of us may still
deep down hanker. The story of our banishment from
paradise and the birth of physical shame isn't – we
can see – just a Biblical story; it is an account of how
we travelled painfully from uninhibited toddlerhood
to embarrassed adulthood.

To make love outdoors is a temporary reversal of the
Fall. It is the greatest expression of confidence in the
wider world; it symbolises that we have tamed the
landscape and we are not going to be attacked by
wolves or harmed by the mockery of others. For most
of our lives, we may have to cower behind double
glazing and heating systems, lock our doors and wrap
ourselves in padded coats, but now we can delight in
a contrastive vision of the landscape as kindly, generous and on our side; the place where we are, for a
time, totally at home. As we penetrate one another
in the grass, we aren't being turned on primarily by
our bodies (we could do the same bodily acts just as
easily, and more comfortably, at home); we're being
excited by our yearning to feel a little more natural
around sex in what is normally an all-too-scary and
untamed world.

We may think it's a bit weird to get turned on by the idea of having sex in a neighbour's garden or in the alleyway behind a bar. It can feel squalid. But more generously and accurately understood, the excitement is far from mysterious and not ridiculous or shameful at all. It springs from a noble and deeply honourable instinct that we easily lose sight of: namely, civilising nature. Sometimes that instinct is expressed via a desire to plant an apple tree and pick the fruit in the autumn; it might lead us to lay out parklands or build sea walls. In a less recognised but equally valid guise, this impulse pushes us to seek orgasm in the open air and thereby to demonstrate that the wider world is our home.

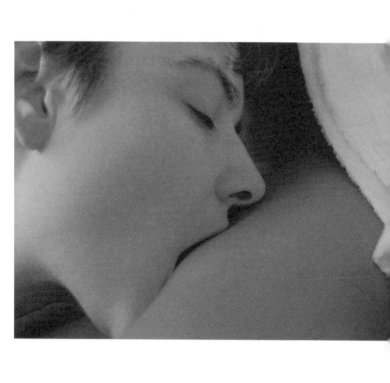

v. Oral Sex

In terms of the person giving it, oral sex is quite a strange-seeming way of enjoying oneself sexually. The mouth, which is normally reserved for speaking, eating, coughing, yawning and breathing, is put into service on the genitals of another human being. Our face is the most personal part of the body, the tiny surface territory we most strongly identify with, by which others recognise us and to which we generally expend the most careful attention. We've studied its minute developments over the years and directed our most heartfelt thoughts while gazing at it in the bathroom mirror. We've lamented an (in our own eyes) imperfect nose or relished a plucked eyebrow; it's what allows us to pick ourselves out in an early-years school photo or see how we're physically related to our wider family group. We're deeply protective of our faces; a hand rises instinctively to ward off the slightest threat. We are hugely sensitive to anyone getting too close to this crucial zone of selfhood.

But now, in oral sex, this face of ours is jammed up against someone's vulva or pressing towards their testicles. In the light of everything we've learned and are, there are few things weirder to connect than a face and the sexual organs.

Long ago, as young children, we might have had no inhibitions around our own genitals; people changed our diapers thousands of times; we were bathed by our parents, sometimes; every part of us from our temples to our toes was equally lovely and fascinating; on long car journeys we had to take a pee at the side of the road and it didn't bother us. Then things started to change. We were gradually informed that parts of our bodies had to be kept concealed and that failure to do so would be dangerous, shameful and disgusting. We learned that many things we might fancy doing – playing with our genitals, opening someone's trousers to have a look, peeping up a skirt – were bad and dirty and deeply unacceptable, and we received horrifying hints that these things could be connected to hideous scenarios of cruelty and exploitation.

We learn to keep our eyes averted from other people's genital regions; we take immense care in changing rooms to deploy towels in strategic ways to ensure no one gets a glimpse of the parts of ourselves we've come to know – tellingly – as 'private'. We come to take it for granted that we cannot be both accepted by society and reveal who we are physically. But, although we generally manage to suppress original free and easy instincts around our bodies, we never forget how nice it would be to be uninhibited and to be the object of another person's lavish, generous delight in all the corners and folds and protrusions of our bodies.

The thrill of oral sex is connected to the brief, magnificent reversal of the generally quite sensible taboos we've internalised. It's a potent symbol of our trust and feeling of acceptance and closeness that with our partner we can do this otherwise forbidden and shameful thing. The act of caressing with one's tongue and lips and gently nibbling and sniffing a penis or vulva breaks down the barrier of loneliness that usually surrounds us. Our partner is in effect saying to us that the usual barriers no longer hold. With me, you can forget about those learned anxieties and prohibitions. With me, you don't need to be ashamed or disgusted with yourself. I am excited by who you are – especially by the parts of you that aren't supposed to be nice and acceptable. The act is physical, but the ecstasy is really emotional relief – because oral sex permits our secret self, with all its 'bad' and dirty sides, to be witnessed and enthusiastically endorsed by someone we like. The privileged nature of a relationship is sealed by an act that, with someone else, would be sickening. The bond of loyalty between a couple grows stronger with every increase in explicitness. The more unacceptable our behaviour would be to the larger world, the more we feel as if we are building a haven of mutual acceptance.

Sex liberates us for a time from that punishing dichotomy between dirty and clean. It literally purifies us, by engaging the most apparently polluted sides of ourselves in its games. We can press our mouths, the most public and respectable aspects of our faces, eagerly into the most contaminated parts of the other – thereby symbolising a total psychological approval, much as a priest would accept a penitent, guilty of many transgressions, back into the fold of the Church with a light kiss upon their head.

The pleasure of oral sex is deeply rich and significant. It isn't primarily about a pleasant physiological sensation at all; it's about acceptance – and the further promise of an end to loneliness.

vi. Anal Sex

For long periods, and in many places, anal sex has been regarded as contrary to nature. In a limited but important sense, this is obviously right. Sticking a penis or penis-like object into another person's rectum does not aim at procreation, which is the primary objective of sexual activity in the animal realm. The anus was regarded as not having evolved to accommodate a tongue, two or more fingers, a length of rubberised plastic or a string of latex beads.

The error has been to suppose that being contrary to nature is a bad thing. It is not: going deliberately against nature or evolution is one of the most important things we ever do. It is not 'natural' for people to recover unscathed from smallpox; evolution left us vulnerable to the bite of the yellow-bellied sea snake; it is contrary to nature to live in centrally-heated houses, to fly in planes across multiple time zones or use knives and forks (when we have beautifully adapted fingers). The fact that inserting something into someone's anus does not lead to procreation is a quality shared with writing novels and playing tennis, which are also interesting and often enjoyable activities that have no direct connection to having children.

By common consent, the anus is the most disgusting part of the human body. It's the most strongly connected to germs and disease-rich outputs. We have developed strict rules about the need for extreme privacy around our bottoms. We take care to shut the bathroom door; it's horrific in public restrooms to sense that there's someone in the next cubicle and nauseating to hear them going about their business. The sphincter muscles tend to clench whenever we feel anxious.

But all this feeds into the tenderness and sweetness of being allowed to explore this part of another person or of letting them do this to us. The more powerful the social barrier, the greater the sense of intimacy when it is lowered. We're not forgetting that the anus is the locus of special disgust – we're relishing this fact. Anal play would quite possibly lose its capacity to delight us if it were regarded simply as clean, healthy fun. If the anus were seen as no more 'dirty' than someone's forehead or shins, its capacity to fascinate us would be reduced. Anal sex would be robbed of its deep psychological significance, which depends on someone letting us do something avowedly filthy with them.

For many couples, anal sex remains off limits even if they have been together quite a while. The sense can persist that this is not a nice thing to do. But this feeling isn't necessarily the end of the matter. Far from signalling something you should avoid, the reluctance might actually be a good target for gentle, generous investigation. It is exactly the feeling that something is wrong, perverse or obscene that makes the mutual agreement to try it so great a mark of love.

vii. Degradation

Normally, and with justification, we hate being degraded and take instinctive offence if anyone says or does anything to us that we feel is even slightly condescending. We are furious or depressed if someone calls us a cunt or a fucking bastard or tells us we're a shit or are worthless. These are the terms people use when they most want to hurt or upset another person, when they are desperate to show contempt or hatred. So, on the face of it, it is shocking and disturbing to think that one (or one's partner) might get erotically excited by using just these sorts of abusive terms in bed.

Calling another person a creepy, sick little faggot or a useless cheap whore, a disgusting pervert or a pathetic, shitty failure is what we normally very much want to prevent. And, although it is unacceptable even to list the epithets, degradation of course extends into political and racial areas, drawing on the gravest, most toxic, insults our society knows. It's not surprising if we find it awkward and alarming – even horrifying – to discover that our partner wants to say such things or wants them said to them. And it can be at least as disconcerting to find we like being degraded ourselves or want to degrade someone else around sex.

We're prone to feeling that it is morally wrong and politically wicked to use such terms. The real-world brutality of certain insults is so gruesomely clear to us that we recoil from using them, and it can seem deranged and almost evil to turn them into playthings. The real-world prohibition around saying abusive things to others might be so dear to us that we are disgusted to think of ourselves or someone we love relishing their use, even in the most private moments of existence. So, someone could be in a loving relationship for many years and never feel they could let their partner know how much it would excite them to have shameful insults hurled at them or how much they long to say wicked things themselves.

Usually, being a plausible citizen in a competitive, demanding world means we have to be very careful about what we say to others, and we have to vigilantly maintain our own honour and status. We learn to be sensitive to what might offend others and take great care to avoid doing so. We become polite, gentle and kindly members of society. But within us there lurk other potentialities. They are rightly exiled from our public personalities, but we do retain somewhere at the back of our minds reservoirs of excitement around degrading others or being degraded ourselves.

The task of culture is not to take fright, but to try to replace fear and shame with insight. We would be wise to begin studying the issue through the lens of perhaps the greatest novel of the 20th century, Marcel Proust's *In Search of Lost Time* (1913). In the first volume, *Swann's Way*, Proust's unnamed narrator, then a teenager, is taking a walk near his grandmother's house in the French countryside. As he passes a building at the edge of the village, he notices, in an upper bedroom, a woman, Mademoiselle Vinteuil, making love to a female friend. He is mesmerised and climbs a little hill for a better view. There he sees something even more surprising unfolding: Mademoiselle Vinteuil has positioned a photograph of her father on the bedside table – and is encouraging her lesbian lover to spit on the image as they have sex, this gesture proving extremely exciting to them both. Early readers of Proust's novel were puzzled by and heavily critical of this scene of erotic defilement. What was this revolting episode doing in an otherwise gracious and beautiful love story, filled with tender evocation of river banks, trees and domestic life? Proust's editor wanted to cut the scene; but the novelist insisted on retaining it, asking the editor to understand its importance within his overarching philosophy of love.

Proust tried hard to make sure his readers would not judge Mademoiselle Vinteuil harshly, going so far as to suggest that even the woman's father wouldn't ultimately have minded being spat on by her lover, so long as he understood what was really going on: 'I have since reflected that if Monsieur Vinteuil had been able to be present at this scene, he might still, and in spite of everything, have continued to believe in his daughter's soundness of heart.' Proust's argument is that defilement during sex isn't what it seems. Ostensibly, it's about violence, hatred, meanness and a lack of respect. But for Proust, it symbolises a longing to be properly oneself in the presence of another human being – and to be loved and accepted by them for one's darkest sides rather than just for one's politeness and good manners. Mademoiselle Vinteuil is, in her day-to-day behaviour, an extremely moral and kindly character, and yet this pressure to be always responsible and 'good' also seeks moments of release, which is what she finds during love-making.

Sex in which two people can express their defiling urges is, for Proust, at heart an indication of a longing for complete acceptance. We know we can please others with our goodness, but – suggests Proust – what we really want is also to be endorsed for our more peculiar and unrespectable impulses. The discipline involved in growing up into a good boy or girl seeks occasional alleviation, which is what sex can provide in those rare moments when two partners trust one another enough to reveal their otherwise strictly censored desires to annoy, hurt and insult. Getting turned on during defiling sex is a kind of thrill at the idea that, contrary to all normal expectations, the other person does still like you, even though you are using appalling language, scratching them and offering to soak them in urine. These are all the things we have been taught, since earliest childhood, we must never do around others; yet these desires are still a part of us that continues to exist and seeks some kind of endorsement. Although defiling sex seems on the surface to be about hurting another person, really it's about asking if they'll put up with us. It is a quest for intimacy and love – and a delight that, for a time at least, we can be as bad as we like and still be the object of another's affection.

For Proust, defilement therefore has meaning: it is a surprising way of trying to improve a relationship. It is not an act of sabotage or a denial of love. It is a deeply curious but, in its own way, very logical quest for closeness. We need to make this kind of move to radical understanding in relation to many things about our sexualities that seem odd at first. We are such complicated and surprising machines, we need to foster the rehabilitation (by which we mean the wise, sympathetic investigation) of parts of ourselves that are otherwise so easy to disown or to panic around.

viii. Uniforms

We often fear that people in authority – teachers, doctors, accountants, librarians, pilots – will be hostile to us, that they will not understand or sympathise with our needs. They will be too busy flying the plane or looking up the scientific formulae; checking the numbers or preparing their lessons; they will instead just make our lives irksome and dull. All the things we want to do will be forbidden and we will be required to be tame, uninteresting versions of ourselves.

A sexual fantasy involving people in uniforms can therefore be an imagined solution to fears around authority. All kinds of uniforms are capable of sparking excitement: most often business suits, but also the outfits of anaesthetists and brain surgeons. These are the professions that scare and intimidate us, but in our sexual games, we invite the uniform in to reduce their power over us. The uniform still stands for authority but now authority has moved to our side, paying us exactly the right kind of attention. The pilot, far from being impassively at the controls, is thrilled to be here with us; she or he is no longer our enemy but our collaborator.

Typically, we associate uniforms with the professional person who is busy and has a job to do: they are pressed for time and have serious things on their mind. They normally indicate someone who isn't so much interested in you as a person as in your blood pressure, the cockpit doors, parking spaces or the legal arguments around corporate tax law. The uniform stands for a stern attitude in which only a narrow range of concerns get a hearing.

By co-opting their clothing in sexual play, one can correct a deep fear that one doesn't matter to serious, busy people; that one can't compete with the demands of the working world. The turned-on pilot or doctor (though worrying if they were real) is a pleasant scenario of overcoming a profound fear of being ignored. Now, in the bedroom, the busy doctor has time for you; the first officer wants to know about your inner life; the police sergeant will forget about your driving infringements; the judge will love you and not merely apply the rules with impartial severity.

The ideal that we are seeing, played out in an erotic context, is that authority might help rather than hinder us, reassure rather than intimidate us. We are, as it were, imagining a utopia in which strength, organisation, neatness and order are there to make us feel more at ease, more relaxed and truer to ourselves.

When we first encounter a taste for uniforms, it can be puzzling, disconcerting – even horrible – to discover. It can feel like a rejection of the relationship: I thought I loved you (or that you loved me) and yet I am – or you are – preoccupied by this apparently strange thing.

This person who is so nice to you when you go for a walk together; the one who is normally fascinating and kindly; who listens sympathetically to your work dilemmas; who was sweet with your sister and who cried when you told them about how your dog died when you were nine and you buried it in the garden.... How can they seem more interested in you wearing a garter belt or pretending to be a pilot than in the essence of who you really are? The worry grows that one has met someone unfit for a relationship.

There is no need for further mystery or shame. The suggestion here is that sexual excitement is in fact fairly easy to understand and not at all contrary to reason. It is continuous with many of the things we want in other areas. Although our erotic enthusiasms might sometimes sound odd (or even off-putting), they are motivated by a search for the good; a search for a life marked by understanding, sympathy, trust, unity, generosity and kindness.

ix. The Gaze of Strangers

At certain points in a couple's life, it may start to seem attractive to invite a stranger or two to witness sex between them. It may in addition be exciting to take pictures of themselves and post them to a website for others to enjoy. A couple might go to a sex club, or a motorway layby, and make love in front of men and women they don't know.

These are not mere acts of altruism, nor mindless perversions. The witnesses have been invited in for a particular and rather sensible purpose: to remind lovers of what is arousing about their partners. We can use a stranger's desire as a spur to help us find our way back to erotic perspectives that have become obscured by the fog of familiarity and domestic routine. We may start to remember the thrill of first undressing a partner by doing so in front of people who will be more appropriately excited by the prospect. It is akin to inviting friends to see a beautiful house we own but have stopped knowing how to 'see'. Their pleasure reminds us of our own, forgotten satisfactions.

The relevant strategy was explored in another context by the French writer Xavier de Maistre (1763–1852). He was wounded in a duel and had to spend 42 days confined to his bedroom – the equivalent, in a way, of getting married and being confined sexually to one person. For a while, he is deeply bored and frustrated. He wishes he could escape and travel to exotic places.

Then he has a brilliant idea. He will take a holiday and go for an adventure, but in his own room, and he records his 'travels' in a mock-serious journal entitled *A Voyage Around My Room*. He treats the familiar items – a chair, his bed, the window – as if they were remarkable novelties. And he becomes genuinely delighted. He is resensitised to objects that had lost their charm. He realises that there was so much he hadn't noticed adequately. He thought he knew his bed perfectly already. But he hadn't properly paid attention to all its different regions; he'd never put his head exactly in the middle and seen what it looked like from there – a kind of soft, blanketed plateau with a little hill rising up at one end (thanks to the pillows) with sharp cliffs on three sides. He'd never looked closely at the back corners of a drawer (although he'd opened it a thousand times to extract a pair of socks); he'd paid – up to now – scant attention to how the sunlight makes patterns on the curtains in the early morning; he hadn't listened carefully to every sound he could hear from the outer world. The key, he realises, is not that something is actually new but that we bring to what is familiar a mental attitude that can make it new.

The de Maistre technique applies in sex when we treat our existing partners as if they were strangers – as if we didn't know them very well already – with the help of the gaze of strangers. There is so much about this person we won't, inevitably, have paid proper attention to. We might never have spent much time looking at their wrist or their earlobes; there's much about their daily life that we don't know: what do they think of when they look at clouds? What item on the news particularly interested them this morning and why? What do they make of the people living two doors down on the other side of the street? Do they prefer cypress or birch trees and what is it about them they like? Large parts of their past are – for innocent reasons – blank to us: how did their personality evolve between the ages of 16 and 19? When did they learn to ride a bike? What was the first novel that they loved? When did they first travel without their parents and what was it like? And we are returned, with renewed curiosity, to the things that first attracted us to them. These qualities haven't disappeared; we've just stopped paying much attention to them.

De Maistre shows us how we can attain a sense of distance – expressed as adventure and exploration – around things and people that we feel (understandably but wrongly) we know too well already. He combats the claustrophobia that comes from feeling we are confined by a situation. He knows that the instinctive solution is to travel, or to have an affair. But since that might be impossible or unwise, he shows how the very things we wanted may be available closer to hand – if only we learn to open our eyes.

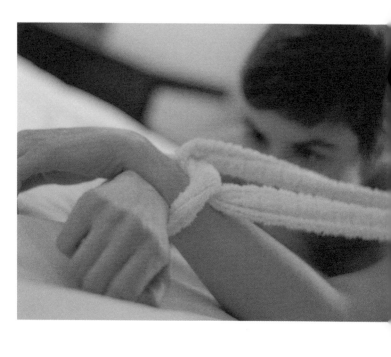

x. BDSM

We have a very powerful and impressive idea of love that focuses on tenderness and respect. We have also inherited an idea that sex should, at its best, be an expression of this love. The union of these ideas means that we are often made uncomfortable by a range of sexual desires that seem to be very far from loving. The wish, for instance, to scratch one's partner, to pull their hair, to slap them, shove them around, tell them harshly what to do – or by the desire to have these things done to oneself – can be disturbing. Bondage, domination, sadism and masochism appear to be an affront to love. Therefore, an interest in them or a fascination with them starts to ring alarm bells: if my partner wants to do this, can they really love me? If I want to do this, can I really love my partner? But when we examine what's going on in our minds around these erotic activities, we can see that they have strong links to the most honourable, intelligent and kindly parts of ourselves. They are not shameful failures of love but important ways in which we may try, with the willing cooperation of our partner, to elegantly resolve deep-set problems of existence. We can explore how this works in a number of key areas.

SLAVERY

We are taught from a young age that we must become independent. We live in an individualistic culture that constantly vilifies dependence and pushes us towards an ideal of solitary maturity. And yet it seems, in our sexual selves, many of us are deeply turned on by the idea of thorough passivity and submission as a form of escape from the over-strenuous demands of grown-up life. Being a 'slave' means that someone else will know exactly what you should do, will take full responsibility, and will take choice away from you. This can sound appalling because most slave owners we can imagine (or even just most bosses) are awful. They won't have our best interests at heart. They won't be kind. So we want to be independent in part because there doesn't seem to be anyone around nice enough to deserve our submission. But the deep hope in the erotic scenario is that we can be with someone who is worthy of our complete loyalty and devotion. It is a common feature of all sexual fantasies that they do not, of course, genuinely solve the problems from which they draw their excitement. But we shouldn't worry if the fantasy fails to solve the problem in reality. What we're looking for is simply a way of explaining and sympathising with the desire.

DOMINATION
Modern life demands extreme politeness and restraint. We have to keep our bossiness in check. In private, we go through life often thinking that we know what's good for another person or feeling that someone deserves harsh treatment. In our hearts, we might like to be very bossy, demanding and insistent. We would like to enforce absolute obedience on all those who

defy us. But of course, in the real world, this is made difficult by the fact that very few people trust us to exercise such power; we simply are not able to rise to the status that would allow us to exercise power as we would want.

The fantasy is that someone else will acknowledge our strength and wisdom, will recognise our talents, and will put us wholly in charge of them. No more need for restraint; no more need to hold our tongue. In the sexual fantasy, someone puts themselves in our hands, as we always hoped might happen. This is an attempt to address the very delicate, and very real problem, of when one is right to exercise decisive power over another person. Now, in the sexual game, instead of this being a situation fraught with anxiety – because one might be mistaken about another's wishes, because there might be resentment, because one might hurt someone – the commands are met only with delight by the person on whom they are exercised.

VIOLENCE

In childhood, we were able to jump around and hit one another a bit and that was fine, even great fun. But now, in adulthood, we are infinitely more circumspect. All violence is prohibited. We are terrified of force, against us or by us.

But in daydreams it can be nice to take a swipe, to have someone hit you; they could get rough; and you could get forceful. It would be violent; there would be a savage edge. And yet, magically, no one would really be harmed. No one would be left bereft. The other person would accept one's extreme possibilities. They wouldn't be shocked. One wouldn't have to be so careful; afterwards there would be love and cosiness, till next time. It is the fantasy that violence is no longer bad for us and others; that our anger and aggression can be expended safely, will not make others unhappy, but in fact will be welcomed by them – and that the fury of another will not wreck our lives but bring us a kindly thrill.

When we are on the receiving end of this type of violence, we may find a parallel pleasure, and a certain sense of strength, in being able to decide for ourselves just how insulted, hurt and dominated we are going to feel. We spend so much of our lives being maltreated by others in the ordinary world, we are so often forced to submit to the malevolent will of our superiors at a time of their choosing, that it can be truly liberating to turn the dynamics of power into our own theatrical performance, to subjugate ourselves voluntarily, in circumstances of our own design and before someone who is, at heart, both kind and good. We work through a fear of our fragility by being slapped and insulted at our command, enjoying the impression of resilience and empowerment afforded by encountering the worst that someone can think of inflicting on us – and surviving.

The bond of loyalty between a couple is apt to grow stronger with every increase in aggression and submission. The more horrifying we believe our behaviour would seem to the larger, judgemental society in which we normally live, the more we feel as if we are building a paradise of mutual acceptance. Such actions make no sense from an evolutionary or biological point of view; it is only through a psychological lens that being willingly slapped, half strangled, tied to a bed and almost raped starts to feel – strangely but genuinely – like a proof of love.

xi. Cross-Dressing

Until very recently, when the internet started to reveal the relatively widespread appeal of wearing the clothes of another gender, cross-dressing was regarded mainly with derision and bewilderment. Cross-dressing (and here we refer particularly to men dressing up as women) could hardly have had a worse reputation. The concept of a man taking pleasure in putting on a pair of stockings seemed laughable, pitiful – maybe even sinister. We assumed a marriage would almost certainly break up the day a wife found her husband in her underwear; and that a manager would lose all authority if his colleagues knew about his enthusiasm for mascara and lipstick. Cross-dressing seemed like an admission of failure. Instead of living up to an ideal of strength, ruggedness and sheer 'normality', a man keen to slip on a dress was taken to be a deviant of a particularly alarming sort.

But in truth, cross-dressing is grounded in a highly logical and universal desire: the wish to be, for a time, the gender one admires, is excited by – and perhaps loves. Dressing like a woman is merely a dramatic, yet essentially reasonable, way of getting closer to the experiences of the sex one is profoundly curious about, and yet has been (somewhat arbitrarily) barred from. We know cross-dressing well enough in other areas of life and think nothing of it. A five-year-old boy living in a suburb of Copenhagen who develops an interest in the lifestyle and attitudes of the cow herders of the

Arizona plains would be heartily encouraged to dress up in a hat, jeans and waistcoat and aim his pistol at an imaginary Native chief so as to assuage his desire to get a little closer to the subject of his fascination.

We should accept that the adult cross-dresser is no different. He too wants to inhabit the experiences of a group of people he is keen on. He seeks to know what it would be like to cross his legs in a tight cocktail dress; to walk across a marble floor in a pair of high heels; to feel a grey cotton bra strap encasing his back; to put a little silver bracelet around his wrist; to feel the breeze on his bare waxed arms and to stroke his smooth long legs in the bath. He might extend to imagining what it would be like to kiss a man as a woman, to feel bristles that are normally his, on lips as soft as those of the lovers he has known. Admiring himself in the mirror in a pair of black tights, the cross-dresser samples the intense, fascinating satisfaction of being simultaneously himself and the object of his desire.

In this, the transvestite is only guided by the sort of questions that we otherwise admire greatly in the writing and reading of fiction. What makes *Anna Karenina* moving is the intensity with which Tolstoy was able to imagine the experiences of a glamorous married woman in love with a handsome army officer. To write *Mansfield Park*, Jane Austen had to learn how to dress up not only in the simple grey frocks of an impoverished sixteen-year-old schoolgirl (her heroine Fanny Price), but also in the braided jackets

of a middle-aged swaggering member of the aristoc-
racy (Sir Thomas Bertram) and the black waistcoat of
a sensitive would-be clergyman (Edmund Bertram).
The balding, heavily mustachioed Flaubert famously
explained to his girlfriend Louise Colet that his heroine Emma Bovary had become for him more than a
woman he was describing as a dispassionate observer
of a fictional landscape: his identification with her was
so total, he felt he had quite literally become her. It was
understandable, therefore, that he should have added
to Louise that he had just masturbated at the idea of
being Emma, lying back with her arms above her head,
on a bed in a little hotel in Rouen, being powerfully
penetrated by the local landowner Rodolphe.

Transvestism is a way of tapping into our birthright
of universal citizenship: it's the most dramatic protest
against being imaginatively bounded by the particular
gender province we happen to have been born into.
Cross-dressing enacts the great philosophical principle
expressed by the Roman playwright Terence: *'Homo
sum, humani nihil a me alienum puto'*: I am human,
nothing human (including mini skirts or a hair band)
is alien to me.

It may be disturbing to sense that one is not so firmly
anchored to the gender one was born into. It may be
bewildering to have to accept that one is at heart, in
the semi-conscious mind, always going to be something far more diverse, multi-faceted but also perhaps
interesting than a mere 'man' or 'woman'.

xii. Rape Fantasies

There are many things that it would be wrong, illegal, dangerous or crazy to do in reality but that we enjoy thinking about doing in ways that are innocent, kindly, safe and very sane. This is very familiar outside of the sexual arena.

As a child, one might have enjoyed imagining going to the South Pole; wrestling and then making friends with a polar bear; adopting a pet penguin with a broken wing; feeding it chocolate cake; getting trapped in the worst blizzard of the century (for one and a half minutes); then spending the night (another 37 seconds) in a cosy, dry igloo before getting rescued by some outlandishly dressed but charming pirates cruising past in their four-masted, nuclear-powered, ship in search of a youthful captain. In the real world, this would be by turns horrific, impossible, dangerous and in breach of maritime law. But in our heads it is lovely. Make-believe is so enjoyable because it takes a scalpel to experience and cuts away everything that would be genuinely awful in the real world.

We understand make-believe when we read novels. It can be delightful to curl up on the sofa, munch a toasted sandwich and imagine being a cold-blooded hitman, an alcoholic spy in the process of betraying their country, the narcissistic, luxury-addicted mistress of a provincial French doctor, a power-obsessed tyrant or a member of a disorganised gang of drug traffickers. As we enjoy these things we don't worry that we're about to turn into the character for real. We're very good at seeing the difference, and there are many safety guards in our minds and in our society that make it impossible for us to do, or even to want to do, these things for real.

After a long, sensual soak, you are lying on the bathroom floor, touching yourself and getting more and more turned on. What if a thuggish character climbed through the window, aching with aggressive lust? They'd not care what you wanted or felt. They'd seize you roughly and force themselves on you; you wouldn't be able to do anything; you'd try to scream but they'd clamp a hand forcefully over your mouth; you'd try to struggle free but they'd have your arms pinioned behind you. Your brain is on fire with excitement as you edge towards orgasm.

But once this story is finished, you might be struck by a wave of guilt and self-disgust. How could you get excited by a scenario that would be abhorrent in real life? When you hear that something like this has actually happened, you feel a savage anger and hatred towards the perpetrator.

But fantasising about being raped is profoundly different from the appalling reality. At any moment you could flick a switch in your mind (or just get distracted by noticing a cobweb on the ceiling), and the mirage would vanish. The character in your mind has no life or volition of their own; they are entirely your own creation. The nice things about being overwhelmed and giving up control and being forced are cut cleanly away from the horrors that would accompany them in the real world. The fantasy has nothing to do with sly approval or encouragement of sexual crimes, no more than enjoying a film about someone who wants to blow up the world means you secretly want the planet to explode.

From the other side, *imagining* forcing oneself on another person can be exciting precisely because one is so intensely conscious that it would be wrong (not to mention deeply traumatic) to do this for real. Imagining being wicked does not on its own suggest one has any desire to really do awful things. In playing this out with a partner one is entirely reliant on the fact that they are having a great time; if one suspected that they were not deeply excited and thrilled, it would be a complete turn-off. This is the diametric opposite of the mentality of an actual rapist, for whom it is decisive that their victim is unwilling and unhappy.

Fantasies around rape gain much of their excitement because they provide a relief (in imagination) from caring so much about other people. Caring too much kills desire; it makes us preoccupied with being nice to the other person, which is at odds with the sources of sexual excitement. The erotic charge of the fantasy does not reveal that deep down we are callous to the suffering of others. On the contrary, it depends on the profound, extensive commitment we already have to the welfare of other people. It's because we normally care so much that it's occasionally exciting to cast off this attitude and briefly imagine ourselves as cruel and heartless.

We can, in this context, briefly consider the phenomenon of impotence. A man is with his female partner. They are kissing and touching, and foreplay is going well. He slides on top of her or she sits up to straddle him; maybe he's already inside her and thrusting away – but then his penis starts to wilt. She looks at him, expecting him to increase his efforts and renew his potency. But nothing happens. He desperately wants to stay hard, but the erection is fading. It's what the French writer Stendhal termed 'a fiasco'. He feels ashamed and desperate. He thinks he's a sexual failure, no good in bed, messed up. His partner is worried too. She thinks that maybe he doesn't find her attractive any more; maybe he doesn't really love her. If it happens repeatedly she might start to wonder what she is doing with this dud.

Often, the cause of impotence is something we'd not initially expect. It's not lack of desire that leads the erection to fail; the man is certainly turned on. However, his desire is joined up with a fear: he's worried that he's imposing on his partner; that she doesn't want him as he actually is. If he told her what he most wanted to do sexually, she'd feel he was horrible and strange. Out of kindness and consideration for her feelings, he holds back from pursuing what he'd really like. He's terrified that she will be disappointed with him and find him unsatisfying as a sexual partner. It's easily seen as a sign of not wanting, but that's usually not the case. He's impotent not out of lack of sexual desire but out of a worry that his desires won't be welcome. Impotence is, at base, a symptom of respect, a fear of causing displeasure through the imposition of our own naked desires.

In passing, this sheds some light on a female experience that to some extent parallels impotence: the feeling of becoming disengaged and distant around sex that is sometimes called frigidity. Rather than being caused by lack of desire – which is what seems to be the case at first glance – a woman may be going through the same kinds of anxieties: the fear that her partner might be disappointed or upset if she were direct about what she wanted. Or maybe she feels that she won't be able to please her partner and out of generosity is reluctant to get him excited. Again, the cause is not really lack of desire so much as tenderness and kindliness – giving so much space to what might not be very nice for the other person that one opts out for fear of distressing them in a more grave way.

The popularity of pharmaceuticals designed to combat erectile dysfunction or frigidity signals the collective longing of the modern era for a reliable mechanism by which to override our subtle, delicate, civilised fear that we will disappoint or upset others. It's actually very touching that we have this problem – it's a consequence of some very nice things about us.

A better, drug-free approach might consist of a public campaign to promote to both genders – perhaps via a series of billboards and full-page ads in glossy magazines – the notion that what is often termed 'nerves' in a man or coldness in a woman, far from being a problem, is in fact an asset that should be sought out and valued as evidence of an evolved type of kindness. The fear of being disgusting, absurd or a disappointment to someone else is a first sign of morality.

This benevolent perspective on impotence also tells us how much ruthlessness can be welcome in sex. Of course, in general, being considerate is a great thing. But around sex, not giving a shit is a turn-on. For the woman, it's a welcome relief from her own self-consciousness – hence fantasies of rape. The point isn't to abandon kindness across life, but to be more accurate in our understanding of where and when it is genuinely helpful. Being unselfish is mostly very admirable, but there are times when we should honour the uses of a little ruthlessness.

xiii. Incest Fantasies

It's not surprising that we have very firmly established taboos against sexual contact with family members. But nor is it surprising if, sometimes, one's fantasy life engages with people we are related to.

An incest fantasy is about, perhaps, a brother or sister. But we explore incestuous fantasies in the company of someone who is not a family member. That's a crucial factor. With our partner we are allowed to safely re-visit in imagination childhood scenes where there was sexual possibility but no action: that summer with your sister in the attic, hanging out with your brother by the lake on a summer night. We've maybe had showers or baths with our parents, or we snuggled together in the same bed and whispered in the dark and it was strangely thrilling. We know all the good, powerful reasons why such things would be a terrible idea in reality.

But now with a lover, you can insert them into a sce-nario. It's fair enough: members of your family have a sexuality like everyone else. Your unconscious has noticed it, and if they weren't related to you, some of them would be just the sort of people you might want to be together with. We should be unfrightened on this score. But there needs to be a huge level of emotional safety with another person to face up to these tricky facts. It is, therefore, an expression of profound trust in mentally repositioning a lover as if they were (for the duration of the fantasy) your daddy or your sister.

xiv. Age Play

There is a fascinating, but also potentially unnerving, fantasy that involves imagining yourself, or your partner, as younger. It might be exciting to think that one of you is still at school and the other is a much-admired teacher; or you are a skiing instructor with a teenage learner; or an apprentice mechanic with a middle-aged driver who needs their car serviced. In reality, this situation might be unsavoury or worse, which is why we might initially recoil from such an interest in ourselves or in a lover.

But the fantasy is getting at important themes. It's about initiation and care. Especially when things go well, it is exciting to revisit in imagination our first sexual experiences, the first kiss, the first time you touched another's body erotically, the first night together. It feels as if something truly astonishing is happening. It's not just true of sex. With many experiences, our first steps are the most vivid: the first time you were able to ride a bike; learning to swim and really feel you could be sure you wouldn't have to put your feet on the bottom; the first time you climbed a mountain or had a conversation in another language.

We can see the same excitement, which we know in sex, being played out in high cultural realms as well.

In the early decades of the 20th century, the Swiss architect Le Corbusier (1887–1965) became extremely

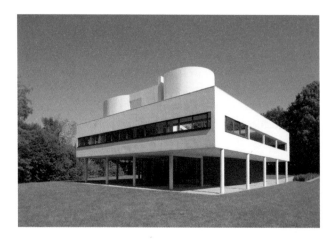

Le Corbusier's Villa Savoye, 1931: revisiting the style of the ancient Greeks.

excited about the planes of buildings – he liked long, straight lines and flat surfaces punctured by openings contrasted with unexpected curves. He felt as if the world had forgotten this since the time of the ancient Greeks. There had been a great architectural initiation in the temples of Athens, but then the world forgot. He wanted to go back and rediscover that early excitement and renew it for the modern age. Like many great innovators, he felt that he was recovering an earlier excitement that had been overlooked. There's a deep parallel here with sex. We might need to go back to the moment when we first discovered sex to reconnect with the true thrill of what we're doing. We were incredibly alert to the drama of what was happening; maybe we felt deep gratitude to our first partner for being willing to do this with us; we were amazed that this could really be happening. Then, later, we tend to forget gratitude and amazement. Sex becomes routine. But it's useful to imaginatively reopen the lovely feelings we had in youth so that they can come to life again in the present.

In the fantasy of age play, we are also circling round very positive ideas of nurture and help. In many areas of life we can see how the right kind of older person can help us with things that are exciting but tricky. They can soothe our fears; give the right kind of encouragement; guide and educate. They understand, but don't share, our worries and self-doubt. We can safely confide in them and know that we won't be ridiculed or criticised. This seems good and important when it comes to studying a history course at college, or getting help with making a daunting public presentation or speech, learning to hang-glide or getting relationship advice – all scenarios where the guidance of a wise older friend can be invaluable.

The same thing applies when it comes to sex: we are imagining an ideal companion for the dramatic journey from innocence to experience. The older person helps us mature. It can feel wicked, but in fact we're imagining what it would be like to be well educated around sex. We know this sort of thing could be very awkward or even awful in reality, but in imagination we're concentrating (as so often) on what could be beautiful and enlivening.

xv. Bisexuality

In a profound sense, few people are truly oriented exclusively to either male or female sexual partners. Just a few people only ever identify as simply male or female. This can be a confronting idea for people who think of themselves as straight and straightforward. Across a lifetime, we build up sometimes quite strict ideas about what it would be OK for us to do erotically and what kind of person we can be around sex – and we might worry what friends, parents, colleagues or perhaps our children might think if they saw us as the more complex beings we really are. It's especially troubling if we are in a relationship, because it suggests a potential interest in people other than one's partner or asks the partner to take on board a potentially unwelcome picture of one's erotic character.

However, we are all both masculine and feminine deep inside, yet have to inhabit just one kind of body. If we had lived in a different kind of society – ancient Greece or Rome, pre-modern Japan or Renaissance Italy – we would, like everyone else in those times and places, have assumed it was normal for people to want to have sex with both men and women. It's not nature that defines the choice of partners but culture.

The expansion of empathy is a general move in the arts. Tolstoy, for instance, loved to take his readers inside the minds and lives of Russian peasants and help them see what might be attractive and good about this kind of life (which would initially seem alien and even repugnant to most of his audience). But at the same time, Tolstoy was warmly engaged by the domestic life of aristocratic families. So, across his biggest books – *War and Peace* (1869) and *Anna Karenina* (1877) – he takes his readers on a socially bisexual adventure, getting them to recognise in themselves the allure of two very different kinds of existence.

Also in the 19th century, the English writer Anthony Trollope (1815–1882) wrote two major series of popular novels, each of which inhabits an opposing political point of view. One sequence (the Barchester novels) take his readers deep into the world view and experience of traditionalist conservatives, while the other (the Palliser series) explores what it is like to be at the progressive, reforming side of the political spectrum. Trollope wrote all his books for a single audience and he was, in effect, getting them to enlarge their sympathies. At an election, each person would only be able to vote for one party. But Trollope's brilliant thesis was that, inside, we are complex creatures drawn, to varying degrees, to both a conservative and a reforming outlook. We are, he suggested, politically bisexual.

People who identify as straight can get access to this part of themselves by asking: if they were to have a relationship with someone of the same sex, who would it be? Not necessarily a real person, but a composite picture in one's mind. What might they be like? In what ways would they be lovely, fascinating, exciting?

This is an exercise in empathy – with a sexual focus rather than a social one (as in Tolstoy) or a political one (as with Trollope). People might open themselves up to varieties of sexual desire that they might not have initially imagined they could get excited by.

The wider examples of imaginative expansion suggest that we shouldn't take this fear too seriously. The reader of Tolstoy who sees the attraction of peasant life doesn't have to give up their city existence and go and live in a hut and become an expert at threshing wheat. Instead, what happens is that an unhelpful fear is diminished; they can enjoyably acknowledge a side of their own character without committing to a life built around it.

We have a range of needs – to be strong, to be weak, to be protected, to be soft and pliant – and different genders might at times speak more loudly to these areas of our psyches. Even if we stick faithfully to one partner for a long time, we can adopt a variety of roles with them and give scope to the mobile range of our erotic imagination.

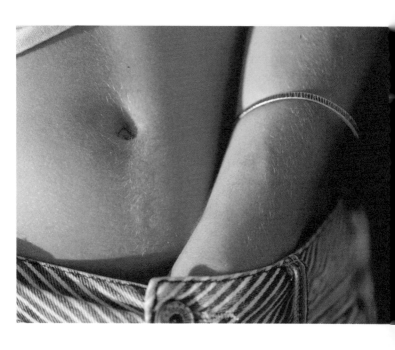

xvi. Masturbation

Until very recently (in historical terms), masturbation was condemned by religions and doctors, and it is still hard to mention in any kind of decent or intelligent company.

And yet masturbation deserves to be honoured as a properly creative activity, a piece of complex mental choreography, which in its best instances draws upon the same faculties that underpin great art. No two subjects could seem further apart. The one: the summit of the human spirit and one of the ultimate sources of meaning. The other: a pitiable, distracting compulsion. In fact, we can identify at least three common moves that both artists and masturbators make as they aim for great art on the one hand and orgasms on the other:

INSPIRATION

For laypeople, one of the great puzzles of art is where artists find their inspiration. To our surprise, it's often in the very ordinary moments of life that artists will identify their richest material. We just happened to see some trees, a petrol station, the view of the city, some countryside; they saw the raw material for masterpieces.

Similarly, the masturbator can be on a train, at the supermarket or in a meeting at work, and – without any outward signs whatsoever – can be discreetly picking up the material – a leg here, a wrist there – that will later be transcribed onto their erotic canvas.

Like the artist, the masturbator rescues people from the everyday, neglectful world, and reveals in them an interest and depth that others have forgotten about.

DETAILS

Much of the power of the best paintings comes down to the way their creators worked at getting the details right. Think of the melancholy and profundity legible around the eyes in Rembrandt's later self-portraits; Jesus's right hand reaching tentatively for his mother in Fra Filippo Lippi's *Madonna and Child*; or the dog with its head turned in unruffled obedience in Constable's *The Hay Wain*.

This attention to detail finds a counterpart in masturbation, where we also lavish attention on apparently minor things that are nevertheless central to delivering an erotic charge. We might, for example, focus intensely on the way the left hand was pressed between the thighs in a pair of black tights; the loose way a thin leather strap hangs around a wrist, drawing attention to its elegance and strength; or the way a pair of glasses hangs a little way down the nose, suggesting a distracted, slightly otherworldly air.

It takes a certain courage, in both art and masturbation, to overcome clichéd ideas of what a painting or session are meant to be about, and instead to go with what one is really interested in – even if it defies certain conventions.

Think, for example, of the way the Danish painter Vilhelm Hammershoi bravely held on to his impulse repeatedly to paint women from the back in grey interiors – just as a masturbator might centre their excitement not on a whole perfect body but merely the sight of a pair of classic black shoes, the left one dangling casually off the toes.

COMPOSITION
The classical theory of painting holds that life will never provide perfection, and that a task for the artist is therefore to edit reality, composing an ideal from the raw material of life.

The ancient Greek painter Zeuxis was said to have requested that the five most beautiful maidens from the city of Croton be brought to his studio, so that he could copy the most attractive parts of each one and then paint the most perfect woman in the world. 'That which is dispersed [in nature] is gathered into one in art,' remarked Aristotle of this story.

There's something of this same manoeuvre in mastur-bation, where the thing we are masturbating about might not appear in one place in life, but where we can condense, correct, combine, add and subtract to get to our goal: we might join those shoes from five years ago to that smile from this afternoon to that rain jacket from the little train station in the Swiss Alps.

We're used to thinking that the way to learn about art is to go to a museum. In truth, we'd be advised to pay closer attention to what's happening during masturbation and especially to the gallery of images that we carefully compose – and often catalogue and store over many years with true curatorial rigour, knowing with the skill of a well-practised museum director just how to pull up a given set of works that might not have seen the light of day for a decade, when it seems to particularly match its audience's needs.

It's on our beds that we can start to understand the role of editing, composition, synthesis and the relation of the parts to the whole.

Not least, we should take a little pride in the sheer ingenuity of our brains as they work towards producing for us highly-concentrated moments of aesthetic delight and transfer at least some of the prestige currently hogged by art over to masturbation – its much humbler, neglected and yet almost equally creative sibling.

xvii. The Love of Porn

Pornography very often feels like the enemy of a sexual relationship. Instead of focusing their erotic desires on their partner, a man or woman gets drawn to online content. Hours are spent seeking the perfect scenario. It can seem (to another person) selfish and rejecting.

All the same, a love of porn is deeply understandable. The business of living is so desperately hard, relationships so challenging, work often so unfulfilling or boring, family dynamics so tricky, and the capacity for honest, kindly conversation so restricted, we may fall into despondency of a kind that draws us to the sudden intense highs offered by short films about lesbians trying anal or muscled hunks whipping each other. Our brains are set up to respond to visual erotic stimulation, which worked well enough when there wasn't much around. We happen to be living at a time when, thanks to technology, the most powerful stimulants are on hand all the time. It's a level of temptation we are scarcely equipped to deal with. We should forgive ourselves, and our partners, for being so drawn to these intense highs.

But a love of porn is more complex than it might at first appear – and actually circles around some important and very good things.

SYMPATHY

Pornography takes our erotic interests very seriously. It doesn't criticise you for being fascinated by threesomes or the idea of kinky librarians or people ejaculating on each other's faces. Instead of saying you are revolting and disgusting, a porn site is welcoming and compassionate. It offers online something we might ideally wish to get from another person: acceptance of the curious ways in which our libido happens to work.

A REDUCTION OF LONELINESS

So often we feel ashamed of our sexual desires because we suspect that they run against what it is normal for people to want. We can easily imagine that we are unusually filthy. We worry about being excited by things that (we assume) no one else likes. In our normal social encounters with other people we never get to see what they are turned on by. Others seem so sane and reasonable, much of the time. We feel alone with our freakish interests. Porn sends out the consoling message that we are, in fact, much more normal than we tend to think. It revises in a helpful direction the notion of what 'normal' actually means.

DISTANCE

Closeness to a real-life partner brings with it many complications that militate against excitement. There's a backlog of unresolved resentments; there's a daily need to put up with this person's less reasonable sides or to be apologetic for one's own failings; there's the pressure to be moderately respectable and civilised. All of these are dampers on sexual exploration, and they fall away around porn. The porn site doesn't care if you didn't take the rubbish out or chewed a bit loudly; it doesn't mind that you slammed the cupboard door or gave a monosyllabic answer when asked how your day was; it doesn't want to go into detail about why you didn't ring your mother on her birthday or take you up on your attitude to credit card debt. Porn in effect says: we don't mind about anything else in your life – just concentrate on this for a bit. Therefore, porn can be a huge relief from the burdensome complications of intimacy. It usefully and blissfully removes sex from the emotional landscape of a relationship.

EDUCATION

Porn invites us to think that there might be a lot about sex we don't yet understand properly. It touches on a range of significant questions: What specific things (scenarios, actions, kinds of people) make me feel aroused? What, ideally, might my sex life be like? What do I need from another person? What can I offer someone else?

Unfortunately, porn doesn't usually provide very good answers to these questions. But the point is that what draws us to porn isn't simply a desire for a quick thrill. In the background we're searching for important kinds of emotional education and assistance.

When we get annoyed with porn for objectifying women or encouraging loutish behaviour or for encouraging inflated expectations we are, strangely, paying it a backhanded compliment. We are recognising that porn influences people and lamenting the particular ways that influence can go badly wrong. We might not spell it out, but the thought is: porn is an educator, just not a very good one. So the conclusion might be that porn should ideally be improved rather than just blamed for its very real shortcomings. Porn is where most of us learn about sex. And that opens the way to imagining a kind of pornography that educates us better.

GOOD PORN

The idea of good porn can seem paradoxical. Many of us are used to thinking of all porn as 'bad'. Yet when people eat badly, we don't try to stop them eating at all; we hope to improve their diet. The aim isn't to abolish food just because some food is terrible. We want good food to be more widely and easily available. The same move could apply to online sex sites. We can't abolish porn, so the goal is to get good pornography. Better porn isn't stuff that's even more thrilling or exciting. It is 'better' in the sense of being better for us – less at odds with the rest of our lives.

We shouldn't be negative about porn, just because of how most of it seems today. In 1800, many people offering medical services were quacks. They didn't know what they were doing. There was a hunger for remedies – however misguided. So 'being a doctor' was nothing like the respectable career choice it is today. What changed was the realisation that we needed really serious, thoughtful and honourable people to go into this field. Health was too important to be left to self-appointed peddlers of fanciful potions.

We're hugely aware of the terrible things that can go wrong around porn in the age of the internet. But the longing for sexual stimulation isn't going to go away. Given how vast the demand is, and how crucial the role of sexuality is in life, it is tragic that comparatively so little talent, wisdom, intelligence, maturity and aesthetic imagination has been directed to it. We've rightly come to fear bad porn, because it damages so many lives. Good porn could help us deal a little better with the complex, tricky fact of being – at the same time – highly sexual and highly reasonable beings.

The School of Life has developed its own porn site, available at: www.pornastherapy.com

xviii. Lesbian Fascination

A man who is interested in women might often find himself getting aroused by the idea of two women kissing, fondling one another, licking each other and doing a whole range of erotic things that might appeal to him. One ties up her partner and drips heated wax on her nipples; they take turns with a strap-on and eagerly perform anal sex. He seeks out online porn in which women do to each other every exciting thing he can think of. A great many straight men are hugely aroused by the idea of lesbianism. If they happen to have a female partner who knows about this interest, she's likely to find it annoying. It seems like a sign of arrogance. Does he expect he's going to be invited to join in? Does she think that they are only interested in each other because there isn't a man around?

There is a more benevolent explanation that sees this fascination as addressing a basic problem of the male psyche – a problem that was identified early on in the history of psychoanalysis. The majority of men, during a crucial period of childhood, believe that their mothers are virgins. It's a primitive, barely conscious, factually nonsensical notion, but it plays an important role. They imaginatively separate their (usually) kindly, intensely loved mother from the alarming, exciting and naughty realm of sexuality. It's offensive to the imagination of the young boy that his mother might be aroused by other males.

If things go reasonably well in childhood, a boy will have many powerful experiences of his mother's sweetness, her tenderness as she says goodnight, as she helps him with his homework and is impressed by the bulldozer he's made out of Lego. She gets him to wash his face, eat properly, not have too many biscuits and listens carefully to his ideas. All these experiences point away from erotic life. He builds a picture of her as pure, devoted and focused on him and as someone who would be saddened and a bit revolted by sex and sexual matters.

This fundamental template – formed around the most important female in the boy's life – is then projected onto other women. The now adolescent boy thinks that if a woman is loving and kind she can't also be very engaged by anything erotic. And at key moments in his teens, it is very likely that this attitude will join up with the idea that females are more reluctant and more cautious around sex than boys. (He's not necessarily right in thinking this, of course, but what matters is what's going on in his head.) This happens at the same time as his own libido is gearing up, he's maybe starting to masturbate and feeling obsessed with sex. This gap between the way he experiences himself and what he imagines women are like creates a lot of guilt around sex. He sees men, especially himself, as dirty and desperate. Sex is a nasty, compulsive but shameful male secret.

If lesbian sex is so exciting to him it is because it proves incontrovertibly (at least to him) that sex isn't just some obscene, primitive, private male thing. The women, in lesbian porn, are shown as highly enthusiastic; they clearly want sex as much and as intensely as men. And they are like this in the absence of men. They are presented as just as carnal and lust-driven as men.

Even if he happens to be excluded from this instance of female desire, the man gets relief from seeing that he is clearly not the only one who wants sex in general. The thrill isn't the assumption that these women really want to sleep with him or that they are just waiting for a man to join them. It's teaching a different, more interesting and more reassuring idea: that women don't need men to become sexually excited. They contain the sources of excitement and (perhaps) depravity in themselves. They're not, it seems, just being reluctantly talked into sex by men. The burden of guilt and loneliness is removed.

ix. Infidelity

After a while in a couple, the idea of having sex with someone other than one's partner can be one of the greatest of all fantasies and prospects, as well as the single gravest threat to the relationship. Monogamy is both a fundamental requirement for love, and may prove a disaster for our chances of ongoing sexual excitement.

However, when we understand the real origins of the desire for an affair, we might be a bit less threatened by the concept and more forgiving towards the possibility. Insofar as we dream of an escapade, the reason is not that we have ceased to love and care for our partner; it is that doing so has brought with it enormous costs to our libido.

Our difficulties around monogamy stem from the way that all of us tend to need carefully calibrated mixtures of two different ingredients. We have a need for closeness, and a need for distance. We want, in part, closeness where we can hug, touch, be cosy, intimate and entirely relaxed and at home with someone. We want them to know our thoughts and to wander freely in their minds too. But we also need distance enough not to feel cloyingly submerged, subsumed or owned by another. We want to retain a sense of freedom, for ourselves and for our partners, and it is upon this freedom that erotic feelings emerge.

In the early days, we were perhaps deeply in the mood pretty much every hour. What was exciting was our ability to touch, hold, stroke – in short, possess – someone who wasn't entirely within our reach, someone who was independent and free to walk away from us, and yet miraculously was choosing not to do so.

Unfortunately, liking someone means we almost always want to reduce their ability to survive without us: in the nicest way, we relentlessly try to erode the freedom of the person we love. Gradually, we kill the very spirit of independence that underpinned our desire at the outset.

We may end up embarrassed and exposed when asking for sex of a partner on whom we are already so deeply dependent in a variety of ways. It can be an intimacy too far, against a backdrop of tense discussions around what to do with the finances and the school drop-off, where to go on holiday and what kind of chair to buy, to also ask that a partner look indulgently upon our sexual needs: that they put on a certain article of clothing, or take part in a dark scenario we crave or lie down in a particular pose on the bed. We may not want to be relegated to the supplicant's role, or to burn up precious emotional capital in the name of a shoe fetish. We may prefer not to entrust fantasies that we know can make us look ludicrous or depraved to someone before whom we otherwise have to maintain poise and authority, as required by the daily negotiations and stand-offs of conjugal life. We might find it safer to think about a complete stranger instead.

In a relationship that threatens to lean towards over-closeness, we can be driven to stray by an urge to prove to ourselves that not everything we do and are is owned by the partner; that we remain desirable to the world and a going concern in and of ourselves. Going to bed with a new person might not be simply about lust: it's about escaping the alarming feeling that one's whole identity appears to be dissolving into a person one otherwise adores.

A stranger bypasses resentments, emotional vulnerability and any obligation to worry about another's needs. We can be just as peculiar and selfish as we like, without fear of judgement or consequence. All emotion can be kept wonderfully at bay: there may not be the slightest wish to be understood, and therefore no risk, either, of being misunderstood and, consequently, of growing bitter or frustrated. We can, at last, have desire without needing to bring the rest of our exhaustingly encumbered lives into the bed with us.

The desire for an affair isn't a sign of evil; it is evidence that we are so engaged in the life of one's partner that we no longer have the inner freedom to make love without self-consciousness or fear of dissolution. Then again, knowing what the fantasy really is may help us to prevent having to act on it.

3

Conclusion

i. What We Really Want Through Sex

At a psychological rather than a physical level, our desire for sex takes us deep into considerations of ourselves as isolated, lonely creatures.

All of us are trapped inside our own sphere of self-awareness and can know others only indirectly and at a distance. We usually don't grasp what they are thinking or feeling; we have to guess at their intentions, and we learn about their dreams and fears only if and when they tell us.

In other words, the Self is lonely. We long to reach out and be united with another individual, to overcome distance and confusion. There are ecstatic moments – usually early on in relationships – when the barriers between ourselves and another fall away. In his 1865 opera *Tristan and Isolde*, Richard Wagner provides possibly the most dramatic musical presentation of these feelings. At a key point, the two central characters fall deeply in love. Tristan and Isolde sing to each other about how they feel that their personalities are dissolving, as if each were becoming the other and they were merging into a single being:

Together:
        ever at one,
        in unbounded space,
        most blessed of dreams!

Tristan:
> You Tristan,
> I Isolde,
> no more Tristan!

Isolde:
> You Isolde,
> I Tristan,
> no more Isolde!

Together:
> No names,
> no parting;
> newly perceived,
> newly kindled;
> ever, unendingly,
> one consciousness;
> supreme joy of love
> glowing in our breast!

Such elevated feelings of love are usually contrasted with lust. But really, lust and erotic excitement are for the most part just equally intense longings for communion that happen to be expressed via the body. The other person's willingness to do the most intimate bodily things with us is the outward sign of their inward acceptance of who we are. They feel close enough and trusting enough to lower their guard and let us into the most private spaces of their being.

We are constantly drawn to the idea that sex is primarily about the body, reflected in our essentially athletic conception of great sex (involving piston-like thrusts and acrobatic changes of position). But at its core, sex is, as we have stressed, a mental and psychological phenomenon. It is the meeting of two minds or souls, enacted with the help of the body. However some of our darker and more complex desires might initially look, sex is not essentially sick and weird. Our sexuality is really built around a longing for acceptance and the communion that acceptance allows. We get erotically excited by deeply tender things – even in the midst of words and actions that look quite aggressive, degrading and bad. We have to find a new way of thinking about our sexuality that is more alive to what we are truly seeking to do in our erotic lives.

Through the 20th century the biggest influence on how people thought and felt about sex came from psychoanalysis. The work of Sigmund Freud moved sex from being a marginal topic of discussion to the centre of the cultural conversation. Freud insisted that sex is profoundly connected with almost everything else in our lives. Unfortunately, he made it sound as if everything else was degraded and made sinister by this connection: you might have thought you were interested in noble things like art or politics, but really, Freud seemed to suggest, you were just being very dirty and base in a disguised way. By extending the range of topics coloured by sex, Freud gave the impression that pretty much everything was polluted by it.

For our part, we strongly believe that sex is connected with high-minded concerns. But the implication is exactly the reverse of Freud's thinking. It's not that when we look at art or politics, we are merely kinky. It's rather that when we think we're being kinky we are actually pursuing some very serious and intelligent goals. Our sexual lives are much more impressive than we tend to suppose – much more deeply in contact with more elevated interests. What seems a bit filthy is actually an endeavour to reach some rather pure and honourable goals by bodily means.

ii. Sexual Skills

If we think of skill in connection with sex, we usually have in mind some kind of technical or physical prowess – a particularly effective way of flicking one's tongue during oral sex or the capacity to have intercourse in unusually strenuous positions. In this book we argue that there's a different kind of skill that's crucial for good sex: emotional skill.

There are two fundamental emotional skills around sexuality that we need to learn: *self-acceptance* and *communication*.

A. SEXUAL SELF-ACCEPTANCE

To accept ourselves sexually requires three things:

1. Insight into what our desires mean

We get disgusted by ourselves when we feel that our erotic longings move directly against the promptings of our better nature. We generally want to be kindly, dignified, reasonable and loyal. But our erotic selves appear at crucial moments to have a radically divergent agenda. In a dramatic reversal of our normal scale of values we find – as we get more and more turned on – that we might want to violate or be violated; we want to slap someone hard or be beaten up; we want to be rough or say coarse things; we long to wear garments we'd not normally be seen dead in, or wish our partner to dress in ways that run contrary to our usual preferences.

When we become sexually excited it can seem as if the most important thing in the world is the right kind of high heels or the muscled torso of our partner – although the rest of the time we'd never give such things high priority. A gentle, thoughtful person might find themselves deeply excited by the idea of encountering a callous thug. There is an infinite variety of individual variations on this theme, but they all point in one direction: the apparent unacceptability to our normal selves of who we are around sex.

The key move here is to examine more closely and more generously our seemingly bizarre erotic wishes. What we are really seeking via sex is usually something very admirable (and entirely in line with the rest of our lives): closeness to another person and warm recognition of who we are. The means might be disconcerting, but the goal isn't. If we can take this point deeply to heart we can see that we're much less divided in ourselves than we often suppose. We're not really going against our own better nature; we're just pursuing it in less familiar guises.

2. A proper, secure appreciation of the gap between fantasy and action

Fantasy, which may be unique to humans, is central to our sexuality for a significant reason. Fantasy stresses what's going on in our minds, not what our bodies are doing. There's a crucial difference between fantasy and acting out. You can fantasise rape, for instance, but that doesn't make you a rapist, or anything like one. It's not that the person with the fantasy is gearing up to do this for real. They're not readying themselves to actually attack someone sexually or be attacked. If during sex we want to be called a useless piece of shit or a heartless bastard, it's not because we genuinely wish someone to see us in this way, and (for instance) sack us from our job, divorce us, or persuade our friends of our general worthlessness. The erotic charge of these words has nothing to do with how we'd usually want to be treated. The real meaning of the excitement is about trust and intimacy: I can risk you saying these things to me because I so deeply trust that you don't think they are true.

We have to be very sure of the other person's real-world regard for us before we can play at having them shout insults at us. The verbal abuse is (contrary to its initial appearance) a search for love and appreciation. Similarly, it is only to our dearest friends that we feel we can safely reveal our most awkward troubles: it's because we know they will continue to be kind and supportive that we dare to tell them about our secret fears, failings and problems. What can look from the outside like a sordid episode is better understood as a deeply honourable endeavour to share the most vulnerable parts of oneself with someone who will understand. What seems 'low' and brutish is revealed to be in fact tender and dignified.

3. A more accurate picture of what other people are like

Comparison is a fundamental source of doubts about one's own normality or decency. One thing that makes us unaccepting of ourselves is the background suspicion that other people – particularly the people we know and like – have more straightforward sex lives than we do. We know all our own erotic oddities, obsessions and quirks from the inside. It can be hard to imagine that other people are like this too. It might feel weird to imagine the carefully suited colleague or considerate friend furiously masturbating or getting excited at the thought of being flogged by a masked stranger or fantasising about being the opposite gender – it feels brutish and degrading to think of them in these terms, even if these are familiar features of our own erotic landscape. Very sweetly, we give others credit for being wiser and more moderate than we are

ourselves. The fatal outcome is that we see ourselves as freakish when we're almost certainly
close to average.

The internet has been a very ambivalent friend
in the search for a more correct grasp of the
sexuality of others. Search engines potentially
reveal that we are far from alone in our particular sexual enthusiasms. But this doesn't necessarily have much impact because it doesn't reveal
anything directly about the people we take the
strongest cues from about what's acceptable:
the people we live with and around day to day.
We can end up knowing that somewhere in the
world there's a band of fellow travellers equally
fascinated by the erotic power of dressing up
as a pirate or having hot wax dripped on their
nipples, but still feel radically out of step with
the people we meet in the real world.

Here, pornography may do us an unexpected
disservice. The people we witness doing things
we find exciting tend to be not at all like us in
other ways. It's as if they are saying: the people who are into these things are like us, not
like you. They don't show how to connect our
normal world with our erotic interests. They
don't say: here's someone who (perhaps like
you) is interested in biochemistry, gardening and
the Renaissance and who is also into fur-lined
handcuffs and spitting. Instead, they seem to be

suggesting that the people who are into these things have no interests or much intelligence outside their narrow area of fetish. So one ends up feeling like a different kind of strange being: a grotesque hybrid.

The solution, curiously, does not lie so much in finding concrete evidence of the sexual delinquency of those one lives in proximity to. Rather it's a move of the imagination and understanding that is required. It means recognising that whatever the outward evidence might suggest, others must be, in their own ways, as complex as oneself. It's a useful act of modesty to give weight to the thought that one is probably not that special. There's a crucial realisation that other people have exactly the same thoughts about you as you do about them. They know you from the outside, so they're not going to automatically associate you with the more wayward contents of your sexual desire. But you know you have these thoughts and feelings and longings. A reasonable, modest logic argues that what's true of you will be generally true of many, many people. Therefore, irrespective of the apparent evidence, one cannot really be that strange.

These thinking-moves change our feelings. They work against the feeling of self-disgust by showing that it is far from justified. By going over them often enough in our own heads we can move ourselves to a more sane and reasonable position: we are individuals, but not terribly odd ones, and we don't need to think badly of ourselves for what are the ordinary impulses of human nature.

B. SEXUAL COMMUNICATION

Sexual communication is often horribly fraught. We would love to be understood by our partners, and welcomed for who we are. We'd love to be able to explain to them what we really want. But so often we find ourselves getting worked up, agitated, defensive or sullen. We go silent, we blame them for not automatically intuiting our needs; we feel hurt that they don't understand even though we feel we shouldn't need to explain. All this is connected once again with the assumptions that Romanticism has made semi-automatic. Romanticism has been entranced by the ideal of wordless communication: we should look into one another's eyes and intuit the depths of the soul. Around sex, Romanticism suggests, if a couple are right for one another their instincts will be magically aligned. Although in reality we are usually very far from these experiences, we still tend to hold onto them as a description of what things are meant to be like.

Nothing sounds less Romantic than giving one's partner a regular hour-long seminar on why exactly one wants them to strut around the bedroom in a pair of thigh-high boots or how (despite being a deeply law-abiding citizen and respectful cohabitee) one would very much enjoy pretending, as realistically as possible, to rape them or have them shout foul insults as one approaches orgasm. The whole idea of having to provide lengthy, complex explanations to a sceptical partner seems almost farcically out of step with our picture of how things are meant to be. However, a commitment to trying to explain ourselves sexually to our partners is a central sign of love: it's because we want the relationship to go well that we have to do this apparently anti-romantic thing: we have to teach them about who we are sexually.

The emotional skill of communication builds around a group of key ideas.

1. Accept the legitimacy of the task

Put yourself in the other person's shoes for a moment: they can't see into your head, they don't know all the things that have made you as you are; they didn't necessarily sign up for this kind of sex (you are asking quite a lot of them). So it's not their fault that they are unaware of certain things you might like sexually and especially of why you like them and what they mean to you. Their ignorance does not stem from lack of love. Their fears and worries are legitimate, however irksome you may find them. Recognising the scale of the task is crucial because it allows us to budget properly for dealing with it. If we can admit that we face a big and fair challenge here we won't expect to get immediate and easy results. Sexual communication is a sub-set, specialised instance of teaching (although we don't typically think of it in this way). A crucial issue in all successful teaching is realising that certain things take a while to get across. We've collectively admitted this very well in some areas: we know it takes someone a while to learn to drive or to master quadratic equations.

Recognising the scale of the task also means it matters a lot when and how communication takes place. We have to choose the moment – probably many different moments – when the stakes aren't too high: not when we're already keyed up and hopeful around sex and want to instantly persuade our partner on some point that feels urgent. We panic and teach badly because we have such a big interest in the outcome. Like any other complex, prolonged educational project, the teaching should take place when it's safe enough for the message not to get across instantly. We need to factor in the assumption that it could take a while, that there will be a lot of tricky moments, and that we might not be very adept teachers as yet. And we need, in some deep place in ourselves, to accept that it's OK for our partners not always to get it.

2. Understand as clearly as possible in yourself why you think and feel about sex as you do

The explanations we give ourselves – the real insights and self-acceptance – are the key bits of material we need in order to help another person make sympathetic sense of us. We stumble around trying to think up on the hoof what to say to explain our sexual interests and desires. We get defensive – and teach badly – when we don't really think that our case is a good one. But if we really believe that we have a good case we can afford to make it patiently and clearly. Yes, of course, they will raise objections; they will have fears; they will have pockets of disgust. But part of understanding and accepting ourselves is that we've already gone through this process in our own minds: we've faced our own feelings of shame, our own worry that we're weird, and our own confusion about whether we can genuinely love the other person if we want to do these things with them, and we've come up with proper answers to them. This is the material we need to dig into in order to make certain aspects of ourselves less frightening and less absurd in the eyes of a partner.

3. Embrace, at times, a melancholy view of sex

One of the severest challenges for communication occurs around non-monogamy and affairs. This might be when you have to not communicate. Tragedy occurs not so much when something goes badly wrong, but when there is a conflict between two good and desirable things that can't go together in the life we find ourselves leading. We want to be open and honest, to share the range of our inner life with our partner. But we also might want – or need – to be adventurous and exploratory in ways that would be deeply upsetting to them.

This idea of tragedy as conflict between opposing ideals has a long cultural history. It was very dear to the imagination of ancient Greece and features in Sophocles' tragic play *Antigone*.

In the play, the lead female character, Antigone, is caught between two loyalties that cannot both be pursued. She has family loyalty to her brother, the warrior Polynices. But she is also loyal to Thebes, the city-state in which she lives. Normally that wouldn't be a problem, but her brother has become a rebel and is killed leading an attack on the city. Antigone wants to bury him with honour, but this goes against the needs of the society, which sees him as a traitor. In this case, it is not possible for Antigone to be both a good citizen and a good sister. The two completely reasonable ideals she holds dear are in tragic conflict.

The Greeks helpfully admitted that not everything we care about can be reconciled. They were heroically honest about admitting how severe a trial this is – how it can bring great sorrow in someone's life. They took the view that the human predicament – with horrible regularity – sets us up in situations where we have to sacrifice one important thing to another.

The mature response to a tragic situation is melancholy – the pained but justified view that life contains some deep sources of sorrow that can't be put right. It's a perspective on existence in which we're not shocked when we have to sacrifice one good thing in order to save another. Being forced into making an uncomfortable choice isn't a curse that we are alone in facing. It appears to be an inevitable feature of any human life and will haunt us however well we may prepare. The 19th-century Danish philosopher Søren Kierkegaard addressed the nightmarish nature of choice in a famous passage in his book *Either/Or* (1843):

> 'Marry, and you will regret it; don't marry, you will also regret it; marry or don't marry, you will regret it either way. Laugh at the world's foolishness, you will regret it; weep over it, you will regret that too … Hang yourself, you will regret it; do not

hang yourself, and you will regret that too;
hang yourself or don't hang yourself, you'll
regret it either way; whether you hang
yourself or do not hang yourself, you will
regret both. This, gentlemen, is the essence
of all philosophy.'

This melancholy attitude, and recognition of a
tragic conflict, might well be the best response
around desires that are too painful and threaten-
ing for one's partner to hear. We have to accept
that there will be barriers to communication
that we can't cross. There will be things we
really shouldn't try to share even with those we
are closest to. We would love to be honest; we
would love to be understood and forgiven. But
we accept the melancholy fact that we just can't
say these things. If we hold back it's not because
we are devious or unscrupulous but because of
a tragic flaw in the human condition – that not
all good things can co-exist – for which we are
in no way to blame.

* * *

Sex is supposed to be one of the great thrills of life – a
source of release, closeness and huge pleasure. But we
also know that often it is linked to shame, disgust,
coldness and disappointment. This isn't something
we're publicly keen to admit to, but it is a widespread experience. This doesn't happen because sex

is essentially wicked or nasty, but because it presents strange and difficult challenges to us. We long for communion but we are also frightened of rejection. We are excited by things that don't seem to sit easily with the rest of what we genuinely care about and the ways we'd like to be.

The solution, we've been arguing, is to start by recognising that sex is an essentially complex thing and that it is more about our minds than about our bodies. In sex we're trying to accomplish very honourable and important goals, but we're pursuing them in ways that shock and disturb our normal attitudes. So we should budget – in ways we don't usually – for the idea that sex is likely to be an area of difficulty in life. When we assume that sex is always supposed to be great and easy we get very worried and panicked when it isn't. The better starting point is the more accurate, more pessimistic, notion that of course sex is going to be a zone that's awkward, where there often are disturbing tensions, where communication isn't easy, and where there are many opportunities to feel ashamed and ill at ease with oneself.

From this less rosy starting point, we can modestly and realistically start to put in place the skills that will help us get things to go better. Realistically, this won't mean that everything will go wonderfully well. We probably won't get the ideal sex lives we want. Great sex is quite rare: so many things need to come together for it to happen. But that's OK; the issue we face isn't usually that our sex lives are just a touch short of perfect and we're fretting about how to add the final little details that will make it everything we could ever hope for. We're starting, mostly, much further down the scale. We're just seeking real improvement, not erotic paradise. We'll still face bouts of loneliness; we'll still meet with incomprehension and dismay; we'll still get touchy; we still might have to keep some secrets and give up on getting things we really want. But we'll be better equipped to cope with the inevitable difficulties and to work our way – fitfully and with reversals – towards a modest but highly important goal: a slightly fuller measure of sexual satisfaction and a few, possibly rare, ecstatic experiences.

Credits

p. 80   Le Corbusier, Jeanneret Pierre (1896), *Villa Savoye*,
         Bildarchiv Monheim GmbH / Alamy Stock Photo,
         © FLC/ ADAGP, Paris and DACS, London 2016

The School of Life is dedicated to developing emotional intelligence through the help of culture – believing that a range of our most persistent problems are created by a lack of self-understanding, compassion and communication. We operate from ten physical campuses around the world, including London, Amsterdam, Seoul and Melbourne. We produce films, run classes, offer therapy and make a range of psychological products. **The School of Life Press** publishes books on the most important issues of cultural and emotional life. Our titles are designed to entertain, educate, console and transform.

THESCHOOLOFLIFE.COM